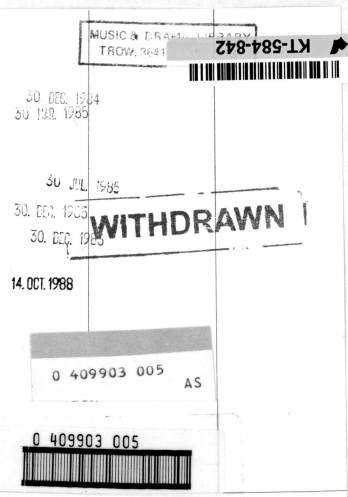

WILTSHIRE LIBRARY
& MUSEUM SERVICE

Headquarters : Bythesea Road, Trowbridge.

ISBN 0 573 00029 8

CONTENTS

This volume contains four short plays, set in the Victorian/ Edwardian era, which are suitable for inclusion in a Music Hall evening, or similar compilation. Each play is tremendous fun for cast and audience alike, containing the essential ingredients of lovely heroine, wicked Squire or similar "baddie" and romantic, slightly obtuse, hero.

In *The Chinese Pendant*, Sir Geoffrey arrives home from the Orient bringing a pendant upon which is inscribed the location of secret treasure. Evil Dr Fu Man Chu attempts to recover it but is thwarted by the British Secret Service.

Every Picture Tells a Story is a melodrama set in wicked Squire Ditchley's house. He hopes to appropriate Farmer Dodkins' farm and lovely daughter, Arabella, by unscrupulous methods and is nearly successful. However, his attempts to make Arabella tipsy have hilarious results and in the end everyone gains but the Squire.

In *Husbands Are a Girl's Best Friend* Clarissa manages to accumulate a fortune by bigamously marrying two rich men whilst playing the dual role of twin sisters. The husbands find out, do the "decent thing" by shooting each other, and Clarissa is left with the money, managing to handle the law as well!

The sad tale of *Maria Marten* is enlivened by the return of her sweetheart Jack (plus false beard) and, just when we think Maria is dead, by the birth of her baby and a joyful reunion for the two innocents.

Easy to stage, with the minimum of scenery and properties these playlets should prove very popular whenever light-hearted entertainment is called for.

THE CHINESE PENDANT

A Melodramatic Thriller

CHARACTERS:

Sir Geoffrey Price, intrepid explorer
Miranda, his beautiful daughter
Willerby Pomfret, man about town
Dr Fu Man Chu, Chinese master criminal
Lotus Blossom, sensuous Chinese servant
Mrs Plumtree, housekeeper
Police Constable, arm of the law
Chairman

Setting: The London residence of Sir Geoffrey Price
Time: Victorian/Edwardian

This sketch has been used many times as a "dramatic interlude" during Old Time Music Hall shows. Introduced by the Chairman as "legitimate theatre" it allows the performers to display their command of the dramatic arts, and if things go wrong, well, we can always blame the stage manager!

H.A.

Running time of the play is approximately 14 minutes

THE CHINESE PENDANT

The scene is the London residence of Sir Geoffrey Price, the famous explorer and collector of Oriental art

A door, the street entrance, is set up L. DR *stands a tall, trailing plant in a large container. Another entrance is set* UR. *A window looks out on to the street. Furniture such as chairs, settees, etc. can be used where necessary*

Miranda, Sir Geoffrey's daughter, enters R *and after fussing around the room, tidying cushion covers, curtains, etc., she goes to the plant*

Miranda I must water Daddy's favourite plant. (*She takes the small watering can and waters the plant*) He is returning home today from China and will be delighted when he sees how it has grown during his absence. (*She replaces the watering can and rings the small hand-bell*)

Mrs Plumtree, the housekeeper, comes on R

Mrs Plumtree You rang, Miss Miranda?

The plant sinks into the container

Miranda Yes, Mrs Plumtree. My father returns today from his journeys in the mysterious East. I am expecting him soon after two o'clock.

Mrs Plumtree (*clasping her hands*) It will be good to have the master back home again, Miss Miranda. Shall I prepare a meal?

Miranda Just a light snack I think, we shall dine later.

Mrs Plumtree Very good, Miss Miranda. I wonder what strange treasures the master will bring home this time?

Miranda We shall soon see. By the way, Mrs Plumtree, my gentleman friend, Mr Willerby Pomfret, will be calling soon. I shall ring when we require tea.

Mrs Plumtree Very good, Miss Miranda.

Mrs Plumtree exits R

There is a knock at the street door. Miranda tidies her dress, pats her hair and poses before calling out

Miranda Come in!

The door opens and Willerby Pomfret enters

Willerby comes down to Miranda's left

   Willerby! (*She extends her left hand to Willerby*)

Willerby takes her hand and gazes at her adoringly

Willerby Miranda! You are radiant!

Miranda pats her hair with her right hand

Miranda (*out front*) Yes, I am, aren't I?
Willerby I came as soon as I received your message. Is it important?

They face each other. The next four lines are said very quickly

Miranda My Daddy's due just after two.
Willerby Is he coming through from Waterloo?
Miranda No, coming into Charing Cross (*as in "horse"*)
Willerby Of course!

There is a pause

   Miranda—darling—
Miranda (*edging closer*) Yeees?
Willerby Miranda—I love you. When your father arrives I shall
   ask for your hand in marriage.
Miranda You have made me very happy, Willerby.

They embrace chastely. Miranda puckers her lips and closes her eyes

   The door bursts open and Sir Geoffrey Price comes in

*Willerby steps smartly away leaving Miranda pecking at nothing,
then losing her balance*

Sir Geoffrey Halloa! Halloa! (*He turns to close the door and receives
   a handful of "snow" in the face. He brushes himself down and
   strides* DL)
Miranda (*moving across to her father*) Daddy! How nice to see you
   again!
Sir Geoffrey By jove! It's good to be home again—even if it is
   snowing!
Willerby (*out front, in disbelief*) In the middle of June?

Sir Geoffrey Ah! Me little gel! Why you look quite radiant!

Miranda (*out front, smiling*) Yes, I am, aren't I?

Sir Geoffrey (*seeing Willerby*) And who, pray, is this gentleman?

Miranda This is Mr Willerby Pomfret. He has been seeing quite a lot of me.

Sir Geoffrey (*out front*) So, this is what she has been up to during my absence! (*To Willerby*) In that case young man, you must do the right thing by me daughter!

Willerby I was going to ask your permission, sir.

Sir Geoffrey It seems a bit late for that! Marry me daughter and make an honest woman of her!

Miranda and Willerby embrace lightly. Sir Geoffrey takes a chain and pendant from his pocket and holds it aloft

And here is the ideal wedding gift for you, my dear!

Miranda turns and mouths a big "Oooh!" as her father places the chain around her neck. She studies the medallion

Tis of no great value, but it does have a curious inscription on the medallion. Probably a good luck charm, may it bring good fortune and happiness to you my dear—and your husband —er—er—(*he snaps his fingers and leans towards Willerby*)

Willerby Er—Willerby Pomfret, sir!

Sir Geoffrey Willerby—er—yes! Not very good at names!

Miranda Daddy, it is beautiful. I shall treasure it always! But where is your luggage? Your portmanteau?

Sir Geoffrey Luggage? Ah, yes, that is with my servant, following along behind.

Sir Geoffrey walks upstage to the door, opens it and is smothered with "snow". He brushes himself down

Come along in! This way!

Lotus Blossom enters carrying two small bags

Lotus Blossom places the bags on the floor and bows low to Sir Geoffrey who attempts a tricky explanation of her presence

This is my fancy woman—er—hand maiden—er—no, servant, that's it! This is my faithful servant, Lotus Blossom.

Lotus Blossom smiles and bows again moving to the left of Sir Geoffrey

Yes, followed me all the way from Hi-Pong!

Willerby Hi-Pong on the river Kwong?

Sir Geoffrey Just below Fu-Chow!

Willerby Near Chang-Kwing?

Sir Geoffrey Yes! You know it!

Willerby (*disinterestedly*) Never heard of it!

Lotus Blossom places her right arm across Sir Geoffrey's shoulders and runs her left hand over his chest and into his shirt front. Sir Geoffrey brushes aside her advances

Sir Geoffrey Later! Later! (*Gesturing with his right hand*) This is my daughter, Miranda. Now Lotus Blossom, I want you to serve her faithfully. And this (*pointing to Willerby*) is her future husband — (*snapping his fingers*) er —

Willerby Willerby Pomfret, sir.

Sir Geoffrey Yes, Willerby — er — thing!

Lotus Blossom crosses to Miranda and kneels before her, palms together as in prayer, and bows deeply. As she rises she sees the pendant and taking hold of the medallion she studies it closely, then steps back, her hands held out in terror. She returns to Sir Geoffrey's side

Miranda Why did she do that, Daddy?

Sir Geoffrey Can't say for sure. Damn mysterious people the Chinese.

Willerby Inscrutable!

Miranda Shall I ring for some tea, Daddy?

Sir Geoffrey By jove, could do with a cup of the old Mazawattee!

Willerby Rather!

Miranda rings the hand bell

Sir Geoffrey And some scones! Can't get buttered scones in China, y'know!

Willerby How very inconvenient.

Mrs Plumtree comes on from R. She gives a small curtsey

Mrs Plumtree You rang, Miss?

Miranda Yes, Mrs Plumtree. Tea and buttered scones for three, please.

Lotus Blossom nudges Sir Geoffrey

Sir Geoffrey For four, please!

Miranda and Willerby glare at Lotus Blossom, she smiles sweetly in return and bows her head

Mrs Plumtree Very good, Miss. May I say how nice it is to have you home again, Sir Geoffrey. And your lady friend.
Sir Geoffrey Thank you Mrs — er — um — (*he snaps his fingers*)
Lotus Blossom Mrs Plumtree!

Mrs Plumtree exits R

Sir Geoffrey Yes! And after tea I shall take a bath. I must get out of these clothes.

Lotus Blossom begins to unbutton his shirt with urgency

Not yet, not yet! (*Out of the side of his mouth*) Later! Later!

There is a loud knocking at the door

Miranda I'll go, Daddy! (*She goes to the door, opens it and looks out*) It's someone for you, Daddy!

Miranda goes back to Willerby as Sir Geoffrey goes to the door. He looks out and receives another handful of "snow"

Sir Geoffrey Do come in, Sir! The weather is most inclement!

Dr Fu Man Chu is ushered in by Sir Geoffrey

Fu Man Chu bows deeply and walks down front followed by Sir Geoffrey

May I ask your business, Sir?
Fu Man Chu You are Sir Geoffley Plice?
Sir Geoffrey At your service, Sir.
Fu Man Chu The famous explorer?
Sir Geoffrey The same. May I ask your name?
Fu Man Chu I am Mandarin of Hi-Pong. I flollow alla ways to London. (*He gives a slight bow*)
Sir Geoffrey By jove! Whatever for?

Fu Man Chu (*pointing*) To Leposess the plendant that your daughter is wearing. She is very radiant.

Miranda (*smiling, out front*) Yes, I am, aren't I?

Sir Geoffrey But my dear fellow, you can't just burst into my home and demand the return of the pendant. I've just given it me little gel as a wedding present!

Fu Man Chu This plendant was stolen many years ago flom the Temple of the Lellow Dlagon in Hi-Pong. I have been sent to lecover the plendant and leturn it to my Tong!

Sir Geoffrey Your Tong?

Willerby What Tong is that?

Fu Man Chu The Ying Tong.

Sir Geoffrey Not the Ying Tong Yiddle Hi Po?

Fu Man Chu The velly same!

The orchestra, or pianist, breaks into the "Ying Tong Song". Order is restored by the Chairman after much hammering with his gavel

The actors recover and return to the plot

Sir Geoffrey But why should you travel half-way round the world to lecover—recover, a worthless piece of oriental brass?

Fu Man Chu It is worthless to all but the blothers of my Tong, it also carries the curse of the Lellow Dlagon, blinging misfortune and death to all who plosess it!

Miranda gives a loud "Eeek!" and holds her hands up in horror. Willerby steps forward

Willerby Allow me to examine the medallion! (*He places a jeweller's glass in his eye and studies the medallion closely*)

Miranda's head is jerked close to Willerby's when he examines the pendant

As I thought! This medallion is of pure gold! And inscribed on the back is the exact location of the treasure of the Emperor Choo Si Yang!

Fu Man Chu Not so!

Willerby And you, my friend, are no Mandarin. You are none other than Dr Fu Man Chu, the Chinese master criminal!

There is a loud chord from the orchestra

Fu Man Chu Velly clever of you to leconise, Englishman! But who are you?

Sir Geoffrey This is—er—um—(*he snaps his fingers*)

Miranda Willerby Pomfret!

Sir Geoffrey Yes, of course, Willerby—er—(*he snaps his fingers*)

Willerby No! I have deceived you all! I am not Willerby Pomfret—I am—(*out front*)—Miles Cavendish, of the British Secret Service!

The orchestra plays the first four bars of "Land of Hope and Glory". Willerby and Sir Geoffrey salute

Fu Man Chu So we meet again, Mlister Cavendish! You have been so clever but not clever enough!

Sir Geoffrey But this time you will not escape, you yellow fiend!

Fu Man Chu How so?

Sir Geoffrey (*stepping forward*) You all know me as Sir Geoffrey Price, but I am also (*he pauses*) "M"—Chief of British Intelligence in China!

The orchestra plays the first four bars of "Land of Hope and Glory". Willerby and Sir Geoffrey salute

Willerby And we are one to two, Dr Fu Man Chu!

Fu Man Chu Not so! We are equal numbers!

Fu Man Chu gabbles into Lotus Blossom's ear and claps his hands. She goes to Miranda and snatches the pendant from her, jerking Miranda's head. She returns it to Fu Man Chu, bowing

So! You see, inscrutable Chinese tuliumph again!

Willerby You won't leave this room alive, you yellow swine!

Miranda Please be careful, Willerby!

Willerby It's all right, Miranda, I have a Black Belt for Ludo!

Willerby takes a step towards Fu Man Chu who holds the pendant up and begins to swing it to and fro

Fu Man Chu Stop! Look into my eyes-sss! You are getting velly sleepy!

Mrs Plumtree enters slowly from R with tea-trolley, which holds a teapot, tea cups and plates

She walks slowly across the stage "hypnotized" by Fu Man Chu

Willerby Your hypnotic powers will not work with me!

Fu Man Chu (*desperately*) You *are* getting sleepy! Walk towards me—you are in my power!

Mrs Plumtree, head up, trundles towards Fu Man Chu. The tea trolley collides with Sir Geoffrey. He sits on the trolley and is borne past Fu Man Chu towards the wings

    Mrs Plumtree leaves the trolley and exits in a daze

Sir Geoffrey and the others are nonplussed by this unexpected movement and stand undecided

Sir Geoffrey Well don't just stand there, help me!

Willerby recovers and pulls the trolley and Sir Geoffrey back into the "action". Sir Geoffrey dismounts from the trolley with his back to the audience but has a plate stuck to the seat of his trousers. Willerby pulls it off as Sir Geoffrey recovers

    Now then, you two! (*He draws a pistol from his belt*) Stand very still!

Fu Man Chu raises his arm to strike Sir Geoffrey who pulls the trigger of the pistol. It does not fire. He pulls again, it still does not fire. He looks at the pistol and walks over to the Chairman, who has been watching the events with great interest

    I say, Mr Chairman! This stage manager is an incompetent fool! This pistol refuses to fire!

Chairman I'm terribly sorry, old chap! (*He walks to meet Sir Geoffrey*)

Sir Geoffrey Look at this!

Sir Geoffrey holds out the pistol, pulls the trigger and it fires, hitting the Chairman in the leg. The Chairman hops about on one foot

    (*Apologizing*) I'm awfully sorry, old chap!

The Chairman rolls up his trouser leg and shows a sock shot full of holes

Chairman You've ruined a good pair of socks!

The Chairman takes his seat and Sir Geoffrey returns to the action, resuming his character

Sir Geoffrey Now then, you two, stand very still!

Fu Man Chu raises his arm once more and Sir Geoffrey pulls the trigger. The gun refuses to fire so he pulls a knife from his belt and is about to plunge it into Fu Man Chu when the pistol fires. He hurriedly brings the gun up and smiles at the Audience in triumph

Fu Man Chu (*clutching his chest*) You have shot me!
Chairman He shot *me* — and I'm not even in it!

Fu Man Chu turns his back to the Audience and sticks a red patch on his chest. Then he turns to the front again

Fu Man Chu I am dying!
Willerby Well done, Sir!
Fu Man Chu (*on one knee*) I am dying!
Sir Geoffrey (*starting his "big speech"*) I—
Fu Man Chu (*on both knees*) I am going!
Sir Geoffrey I—

Fu Man Chu is now on one side on the floor

Fu Man Chu I am going!
Sir Geoffrey (*pushing Fu Man Chu down with his foot*) He is gone!

Fu Man Chu dies

I have rid the world of a monster! Never again shall his evil powers terrorize nation after nation!

Sir Geoffrey blows smoke from the barrel of his pistol as the orchestra plays a chord

Willerby Well done, Sir!
Miranda Bravo, Daddy!
Sir Geoffrey And now for his accomplice! Lotus Blossom!

Willerby steps across and raises Lotus Blossom's coolie hat, looking into her face

Willerby This is no Lotus Blossom — this is Limehouse Lil! The police have been after her for years!
Miranda Call a constable!

Sir Geoffrey goes to the door, opens it and receives another handful of "snow" as he blows a police whistle

Sir Geoffrey The police will soon be here! (*He brushes the "snow" off and closes the door*)

There is an awkward pause as they all face the outer door, waiting for the Constable

Eventually the Constable comes on R, *behind them*

Constable Hello! Hello! Hello!

Everyone does an "about-turn" to face him

Sir Geoffrey Ah, Constable, arrest this woman! She is none other than Limehouse Lil, do your duty!

The Constable grabs Miranda

Constable Yes, Sir! Come on, Lil! Down the nick, double quick!
Willerby Not her, you fool! That one over there!
Constable (*releasing Miranda and saluting*) Sorry, Miss! (*He goes to Lotus Blossom*) Cummer—longa—me, Lil!
Lotus Blossom Oh, officer! I am innocent! I will do anything for my freedom!
Constable Anything? (*He grins at the Audience*) This could be my lucky day! (*He puts an arm round Lotus Blossom's waist and leads her to the door. He turns and salutes*) Evening all!

The Constable and Lotus Blossom exit, closing the door

Sir Geoffrey Well done, young fella me lad! What *is* your name? (*He snaps his fingers*)
Willerby Willerby P—
Miranda No! Miles Cavendish!
Willerby So it is!
Sir Geoffrey Well, whatever it is, well done!

Sir Geoffrey and Willerby shake hands as Miranda goes to the tea-trolley

Miranda Anyone for tea?
Sir Geoffrey Rather!
Miranda (*pouring tea*) It's rather weak!

Miranda pours the tea into the plant container. The plant immediately "grows" to its original height again

As they watch the plant grow, Fu Man Chu stirs and lifts his head

Fu Man Chu I am going!

Sir Geoffrey rushes over and holds him down with a foot

Sir Geoffrey We British have triumphed again!

Sir Geoffrey holds a struggling Fu Man Chu down as Willerby and Miranda embrace distantly. "Land of Hope and Glory" is heard from the orchestra as the Curtain falls, and it continues during curtain calls and tableaux

First Curtain Tableau. Sir Geoffrey holds down Fu Man Chu with his foot; Willerby and Miranda are in a very passionate clinch. The Constable and Lotus Blossom have exchanged coolie hat and helmet and are also in a tight embrace. They realize that the Curtain has opened and "break", and stand facing front for an embarrassed curtain call

Second Curtain Tableau. Sir Geoffrey and Fu Man Chu have hands at each other's throat; the Constable has Miranda in an embrace and Willerby has Lotus Blossom in a tight clinch. They break as Curtain opens and smile at the Audience but resume "action" before the Curtain closes

CURTAIN

FURNITURE AND PROPERTY LIST

On stage: Essential items:
Plant in large container (see Property notes)
Watering can
Settee with cushions
Curtains at window
Table. *On it:* small hand bell

Off stage: Two bags **(Lotus Blossom)**
Tea trolley. *On it:* Teapot, cups, saucers, plates, sticky plate (see Property notes), etc. **(Mrs Plumtree)**

Personal: **Sir Geoffrey:** chain and pendant; gun; knife; police whistle
Willerby: jeweller's glass
Chairman: sock full of holes
Fu Man Chu: red patch (with velcro)

LIGHTING PLOT

To open: Interior lighting
No cues

EFFECTS PLOT

Orchestra music cues not included

Cue 1   **Sir Geoffrey** turns to close door   (Page 4)
"Snow" is thrown in his face

Cue 2   **Sir Geoffrey** opens door   (Page 5)
"Snow" is thrown in his face

Cue 3   **Sir Geoffrey** goes to the door   (Page 7)
"Snow" is thrown in his face

Cue 4   **Sir Geoffrey** goes to the door to blow police whistle   (Page 11)
"Snow" is thrown in his face

COSTUME PLOT

Sir Geoffrey: tropical kit—khaki shirt and shorts, socks and boots. Sam Browne belt and holster. (A struggle to withdraw pistol whilst repeating the line "Stand very still" can get an added laugh)

Willerby: A "Gatsby"-type suit with wing collar and spats. Or a striped blazer and white flannels with boater. A cane and gloves can be used with the suit

Miranda: Victorian/Edwardian-type high-necked dress

Fu Man Chu: Black gown or cloak with a high neck. Black skull cap with pigtail. Long moustache

Lotus Blossom: Oriental dress with skirt slit to waist revealing long shapely leg. Coolie-type hat with pigtail. Slant-eyed make-up

Mrs Plumtree: black dress, white apron and cap

Constable: police uniform of the correct period

PROPERTY NOTES

Plant   This can be made from green rope or cord with paper or plastic leaves. Weighted at the bottom and held up by nylon thread over a pulley it can "grow" or "die" at will.

Sticky plate   This can be a genuine "sticky" plate or paper plate with string through the centre. As Sir Geoffrey sits on the trolley he pulls the string up between his legs thus holding plate on to the seat of his trousers.

EVERY PICTURE TELLS A STORY

A Melodrama

CHARACTERS:
Arnold, a lecherous butler
Squire Ditchley, an unscrupulous landowner
Arabella, an unspoilt country maid
Farmer Dodkins, her simple father

Setting: the drawing-room of Squire Ditchley's house

Running time approximately 12 minutes

EVERY PICTURE TELLS A STORY

The scene is the drawing-room of wicked Squire Ditchley's house

The butler, Arnold, a short, hunchbacked man with a slight limp, enters with a tray of glasses and a bottle of Napoleon brandy. He moves aside a vase of flowers on the table and places the tray there

Arnold (*to the Audience*) All is ready! For today's the day! Another black mark in my master's book as he puts the squeeze on one more landowner and adds yet another farmstead to his rapidly growing estate. A hard, unscrupulous man is my master, Squire Ditchley. The biggest landowner for miles around and becoming a powerful figure in the county! He is fast becoming a rich man — if only I could get my hands on some of his ill-gotten gains! (*He runs a hand over the brandy bottle, looks both ways and pours himself a small measure and sips slowly*) Today he forecloses the mortgage on Honeybrook Farm at two o'clock and old Farmer Dodkins and his daughter Arabella will be turned out into the lane with their few bits and pieces! (*He rolls the glass between his hands, finishes his drink, and replaces the glass on the tray*). I have no sympathy for old Dodkins — but his daughter Arabella! (*He snorts and holds his hands cupped before his chest*) The trimmest pair of ankles I have ever seen! But she would not even notice a poor twisted figure such as I! (*He reaches for the brandy as a voice calls off*)

Squire (*off*) Arnold! Arnold! Where are you?

Arnold steps smartly away from the tray

   Squire Ditchley enters R

The Squire throws his stick to Arnold, who catches it. As the Squire crosses L *he lobs his hat on to the stick. Arnold follows him, dusting the Squire's jacket with a brush taken from his tunic pocket*

   That's enough! Who were you talking to? I could hear voices!
Arnold 'Twas only meself, Master! I was humming!
Squire (*sniffing at the butler*) So you are! As always! Is all ready?

Arnold (*gesturing to the tray*) As you requested — real Napoleon brandy.

Squire Good! (*Rubbing his hands*) Just after two o'clock my faithful servant, we shall be celebrating! Honeybrook Farm shall be mine!

Arnold You're the cunning one, Master. This will be the fifth farm in six months that you have stolen — acquired!

Squire And there's more to come — you shall see! Soon the Ditchley estate shall encompass half the county!

Arnold lays the stick and hat across a chair and comes down front

Arnold As we seem to be more affluent these days, Master, do you think you could rustle up some of my back pay?

Arnold cups his right hand beside his body hoping for a windfall. The Squire slaps his hand and sends it swinging round like a propeller

Squire You ungrateful wretch!

Arnold stops his arm revolving and cringes away from his master, step by step until he is almost into the wings

Squire You've a steady job and a bed to sleep in! Next thing, you'll be wanting a day off!

Arnold Oh, no, Master! I wouldn't dream of it —

Squire Think yourself lucky you've a roof over your head — there's some today who will be turned into the street! Ha! Ha! Ha!

Arnold (*to the Audience*) I told you he was hard, didn't I? (*To the Squire*) Do you mean to turn out old Dodkins and his daughter?

Squire The farmer has until two o'clock to repay his debt — what time is it now, Arnold?

Arnold feels in his waistcoat for his watch, then puts a hand to his ear

Arnold Why, the clock chimes now! Listen, it's two o'clock!

The drummer strikes a cow-bell three times. Arnold and the Squire glare at him

Squire Time is up! (*He rubs his hands*) Honeybrook Farm is mine at last!

Arnold shakes his head in sorrow

Arabella (*off; loudly*) Yoo-hoo!

Squire But who can this be? Is it the farmer?

Arnold (*peering off* L) No, Master. It's the farmer's daughter, Miss Arabella. The toast of the village tabernacle!

Squire You keep your lustful eyes off her, you old fool! As I possess Honeybrook Farm, so shall I possess Miss Arabella!

Arnold You don't mean—

Squire But I do—her father can apply at the poor-house. But I shall offer her shelter and comfort in return for—Ha! Ha! Ha!

Arnold (*to the Audience*) There'll be no holding him now!

Arabella hurries on, wearing a long summer dress and broadbrimmed hat

Arabella Mr Ditchley, am I in time? Is it past two?

The Squire walks to meet her. He takes her hand and smiles sweetly

Squire Why, me chee-ild. Tush! Tush! Time stands still when you are by my side!

Arabella (*blushing*) Mr Ditchley—

Squire Please call me Randolph.

Arnold (*to the Audience*) She doesn't stand a chance!

Arabella Very well—Randolph. My father comes to keep his appointment, but he walks so slowly (*to the Audience*)—his arthritis, you know—

Squire Tell me, child, does he bring the money?

Arabella (*downcast*) Alas! We are without funds.

Squire (*aside*) Good! (*He moves in closer to Arabella*) Then we can discuss our future friendship—(*He puts his arm round Arabella's waist*)

Arabella Our friendship?

Squire Yes, over a glass of something.

Arnold (*to the Audience*) Here we go!

The Squire takes Arabella to C *as Arnold collects the tray from the table and joins them to Arabella's* L

Arabella (*eyeing the bottle*) But, Sir, I must not drink strong liquor! What would the children at the tabernacle say!

Squire Have no fear, me dear! 'Tis but a fruit cordial made by a maiden Aunt!

Arnold Aunt Napoleon! (*He expertly holds the tray on one hand and pours from the bottle with the other*) Say when!

Squire Right after this drink!

The Squire and Arabella each take a glass

Bottoms up!

Arabella puts hand to mouth upon hearing such a naughty word. They drink. The Squire sips, Arabella downs hers in one gulp

Arabella Weeeeeh! (*She shakes her head*) What a lovely drink! Daddy's fruit cordial never tasted like this! (*She thrusts out her glass for a refill*)

Arnold tops up her glass, shaking his head

Arnold It won't be long now!

Arabella drinks. Fortified, she approaches the Squire

Arabella Mr Ditchley — er — Randolph. I have come to plead for Daddy!
Arnold Poor little pleader!
Squire 'Tis too late, me dear. 'Tis past two o'clock.
Arabella I want to speak on his behalf. If you turn us out from the farm, we shall have nowhere to go! And I would do *anything* to help Daddy!

The Squire's eyebrows shoot up

Arnold Steady, lad!
Squire Let me put a proposition to you, my dear. As your father no longer owns the farm, may I offer you a position?

Arabella's eyes pop open

As my housekeeper?

Arabella finishes her drink as he speaks, then rubs her fingers round the inside of the glass and licks it loudly

Arabella But what about the tabernacle?
Arnold There'll be no tabernacle tonight!

Arabella looks closely into her glass with one eye, then hiccups loudly and violently

Arabella Hic! Hic! Hic! Parn me! (*She sways from side to side*)

Arnold and the Squire totter with her, afraid that she may fall

Dodkins (*off*) Arabella! Arabella! Are you there?

Squire It's the farmer!—He mustn't find her like this—hide her behind the curtain!

The Squire and Arnold take Arabella, and with difficulty hide her behind a curtain — or off stage — to R, then resume their positions midstage

> *Farmer Dodkins, leaning heavily upon a walking stick and holding his aching back, enters from R*

Dodkins Good afternoon, Squire! Is my little Arabella here?

The Squire and Arnold go through a prolonged search of the room, under chairs and table, behind pictures, etc. Arnold removes flowers from the vase and peers inside. They both feel their pockets, the Squire opening his jacket and looking under his arm-pits, just to be sure

Squire No, she doesn't seem to be here, Dodkins! Have you seen her, Arnold?

Arnold No, Master, not a whisper!

Arnold nods his head in the direction of the hidden Arabella. Dodkins stares blankly

Dodkins Have you got the twitch?

Squire Why the concern for your daughter, Dodkins?

Dodkins She ran on ahead of me, Squire, I'm very slow these days—(*to the Audience*)—it's me arthritis, you know. We come to talk about the farm.

Squire Huh! She hasn't been here, and you are too late, the farm is now mine!

Dodkins Oh, dear, oh, dear! Now that's not like my little Arabella. She is such a sweet child. (*He ponders*)

> *Arabella sways on from behind the curtain, pours another drink, sips, waves weakly to her father and sways off, unseen by the others*

Squire You are well aware of the terms of your mortgage, Dodkins—

Dodkins But I can't see the small print so clearly these days—(*to the Audience*)—my eyes ain't what they used to be!

Squire It was a simple case of pay out, or get out! And don't come bleating to me about your aches and pains, you old goat. (*He *studies his fingernails*) Honeybrook Farm is now my property! Good day, Dodkins!

Dodkins prepares to give a big speech to the Audience. During his speech Arnold takes out a handkerchief and dabs his eyes

Dodkins Your property? But I lived and worked there, man and boy, these fifty-seven years. I ploughed and reaped, and raked and sown, come rain, come shine, day in, day out. And now—

Arabella staggers on with a half-pint glass, hat askew, goes for the bottle, misses it, gets it the second time, sloshes some liquid in the glass, takes a swig, waves fingers at her father and staggers off behind the curtain, unseen by the others

—just because I can't pay the last instalment of me mortgage I'm to be turned out, all for three pounds, two and tuppence!

Dodkins shakes his head in disbelief. Arnold thrusts his hand into his pocket and takes out his small change. He quickly checks and shakes his head at the farmer. The Squire is unmoved, he strokes his moustache and looks away disinterestedly

What a calamity! Finished! Bankrupt!

Squire The Bailiff is on his way, Dodkins, collect your bits and pieces and go!

Dodkins Turned out into the lane at my time of life! Where shall I go? And all for three pounds, two and tuppence!

Arnold checks his inside jacket pocket and shakes his head, wiping his eyes

I don't mind for myself—but what is to become of my little Arabella? (*He smiles*) Ah! But as long as I have her to lean on I shan't go far wrong—

As he speaks Arabella comes lurching on. Hat on back of head, holding a pint tankard she makes a long slanting detour before she reaches the bottle. She sloshes some drink into the tankard, spills some, sweeps it off the table with her hand into the glass and, with a brief flutter of the hand, she lurches back behind the curtain

—she's a great comfort to me is my little Arabella. A pure, unspoiled, sweet lass, with lovely blue eyes—

Arnold cups his hands before his chest and snorts

— the leading hymn singer at the local tabernacle, y'know. I wonder what hymn it will be tonight?

Arnold (*nodding towards the Squire*) Him over there, the way things are going!

Dodkins I must do something if only for poor Arabella's sake!

Squire It's too late, Dodkins! Send the old duffer on his way, Arnold!

Dodkins It's never too late! I have one prized possession that I cherish above all else, this I would gladly surrender to you in exchange for the deeds of Honeybrook Farm!

The Squire mimes the female figure with his hands, his face lighting up

Squire He strikes a hard bargain, but if there is one thing I desire more than Honeybrook Farm, it is — (*he mimes the female form again*) I might consider such a transaction, Dodkins. Who — er — what might this prized possession be, hm?

Dodkins Why this, Squire —

Dodkins exits and returns immediately with a framed oil painting

— 'Tis been in our family for generations!

Squire A painting? Huh! (*He folds his arms and looks away in disgust*)

Arnold steps forward and, taking out a magnifying glass, studies the painting. He takes it from Dodkins and goes over to the Squire

Arnold Master! It's painted by some geezer called "Rembrandt". Ever heard of him?

Squire Rembrandt? (*Quickly*) It's not?

Arnold (*quickly*) It is!

Squire (*quickly*) You sure?

Arnold (*quickly*) My life!

Squire (*quickly*) My word! (*Calmly*) How much are you asking, Dodkins?

Dodkins They do say it's worth a small fortune — but all I ask is for three pounds, two and tuppence. Take the painting in exchange for the deeds of Honeybrook Farm!

Squire Very well! It's a deal!

The Squire takes the deeds from an inside pocket and he holds the painting while Arnold hands the deeds to the farmer, who is delighted

Dodkins Saved at last! If only Arabella were here to share this moment!

Arabella, in a very dishevelled state, crawls from behind the curtain

She crawls to the table. She takes the vase, grasps hold of the flowers and hurls them over her head and empties the rest of the brandy into the vase. She struggles to her feet as the dialogue continues

The Squire is studying the painting with Arnold

Squire It must be worth every penny of five thousand pounds. A small fortune in exchange for a dilapidated farmhouse! Ha! Ha! A most rewarding afternoon!

Arnold 'Ere! I spotted the artist's name! (*He cups a hand down by his leg to receive a tip*)

Squire All right! You shall have a small reward, when I have some small change!

Arnold (*to the Audience*) I knew he *was* one — but I didn't know he was a *tight* one!

Dodkins studies the deeds with great pleasure. Arabella is now on her feet with the vase of brandy

Squire Get rid of the farmer, Arnold. For now I shall have my pleasure with Miss Arabella!

Arnold hesitates

Go on! Chuck him out!

Arnold (*to Dodkins*) I'm sorry, guv'nor, but you'll have to go. The Squire has some unfinished business to attend to.

Dodkins (*pointing to the deeds*) My Arabella will be overwhelmed!

Arnold (*glancing at the Squire*) More than likely!

As Dodkins turns to leave, Arabella, after a lurching walk from the table, pushes herself between her father and Arnold, holding out the vase and with a silly grin on her face. The three men are shocked by her appearance

Arabella Hello, Daddy!

Dodkins Arabella! (*He gasps*)

Arabella (*pinching Arnold's cheek*) Hello, chubby-chops!

Arabella staggers towards Arnold who, with obvious pleasure grasps her tightly round the waist with both arms. He smiles out front

Arnold Me luck's changed! (*He snorts*)

Dodkins Arabella! Are you ill?

Arabella Ill? I've never felt better in my life!

Arnold Neither have I!

Arabella (*holding out the vase*) Try some buttercup cordial, Daddy, get rid of your arthri—arthit—backache!

Dodkins (*sniffing the vase*) Why, 'tis strong drink, Arabella! Lord above, girl! Why, you're drunk!

Arabella stands upright, away from Arnold, with a sober expression

Arabella Me drunk? Never! (*She staggers*) Me—the pride of the nabertackle—(*hic*)—tabercackle (*hic*). Are you suggesting that I am under the alfluence of incorhole?

Dodkins You are positively pie-eyed! If I find the rascal that did this to you I shall be after him with me sickle!

The Squire pulls his coat-tails round as protection

Squire Out with them, Arnold! That simpering old fool—and his brandy-sloshing daughter!

Arabella hoists her skirts and looks at her legs

Arabella Who's got bandy stockings?

Arnold Brandy! Brandy! In the glass!

Arabella Is it?

Arabella lurches towards the Squire. He holds the painting between himself and Arabella

Hello, Randy! Have some brandy!

As Arabella advances with the vase in her right hand before her it bursts through the painting and the vase is thrust up into the Squire's face

Drink up, Randy!

Squire Look at my painting! Five thousand pounds up the spout!

Arabella Clumsy me. (*She reaches round the frame with her left hand and recovers the vase*) Sorry about that.

Dodkins Come along, Arabella! I must get you into bed!

Arnold Allow me to help you!

Arnold holds Arabella by the waist, and walks her L. Arabella puts her arm across his shoulders

Arabella Come on, chubby-chops. I'll show you the way!

Squire Arnold, what shall we do?

Arnold I don't know about you, guv'nor, but I'm going to be busy!

Arnold and Arabella lurch off together singing "Show Me The Way To Go Home"

Dodkins You shall pay for this outrage, Ditchley!

Dodkins stomps off L after the others

Squire Pay for it? *Pay* for it? I've paid more than enough! No farm—no Arabella—no butler! And now—no painting! (*He punches the remainder of the canvas from its frame, hangs the frame round his neck and with a mincing walk down front, "a la Bruce Forsyth"*) Never mind! Nice frame! Nice frame!

CURTAIN

FURNITURE AND PROPERTY LIST

Only essential furniture is listed. Other items can be added as required

On stage: Table. *On it:* vase of flowers
Chairs
Curtains at window
Pictures on walls

Off stage: Tray. *On it:* glasses and bottle of Napoleon brandy **(Arnold)**
Oil painting in gold frame **(Dodkins)**
Half-pint glass **(Arabella)**
Pint tankard **(Arabella)**

Personal: **Squire:** stick, estate deeds
Arnold: brush, magnifying glass
Dodkins: stick

LIGHTING PLOT

An interior setting

No cues

EFFECTS PLOT

No cues

HUSBANDS ARE A GIRL'S BEST FRIEND

A Victorian Comedy

CHARACTERS:
Lord Rampart, a pillar of society
Branston, the butler
Lady Clarissa Rampart, Rampart's angelic wife
Mrs Cullet, her sensuous twin sister
Mr Cullet, her outraged husband
Constable, thick arm of the law

Setting: the London home of Lord Rampart

Time: Victorian

Running time approximately 13 minutes

PRODUCTION NOTE

The parts of Lady Clarissa and Mrs Cullet, the twin sisters, are played by the same actress. Clarissa, pure, modest and of angelic character, contrasts vividly with Mrs Cullet, a lady of above average physical attractiveness and of very sensuous behaviour. Mrs Cullet's low-cut gown can be worn all through the action and when Clarissa is on a cloak can be worn over it as she is, of course, either departing or arriving at the house. During the final moments, when the Constable is on, she can remove the cloak and assume her Mrs Cullet character in tempting the Constable

HUSBANDS ARE A GIRL'S BEST FRIEND

The scene is the London home of Lord Rampart, member of the House of Lords and celebrated art collector

Lord Rampart, just returned from the House, enters L. He glances at his gold hunter and rings the small hand bell which is on the table C

Branston, the butler, enters L. He is rather bent in stance and has a staggering, lurching walk

Branston halts beside Lord Rampart. The latter straightens Branston's stance. This is accompanied by a rattle-clicking effect from the orchestra (or off)

Branston You rang, me Lord?

Rampart Yes, Branston. Please inform her Ladyship that I am returned from the House and ask cook to have luncheon ready in forty minutes.

Branston Very good, me Lord.

Branston staggers and lurches off in a roundabout route

Rampart lights a cigarette and studies a magazine

Branston enters again from L

Branston Me Lord. Her Ladyship will be joining you in a few moments.

Rampart Thank you, Branston. That will be all.

Branston Very good, me Lord.

Branston lurches towards the exit in his roundabout way

Lady Clarissa Rampart enters and stands in the doorway. She wears a cloak

Branston collides with her and staggers back several paces before resuming his exit

Branston exits

Clarissa goes to greet her husband

Clarissa Archibald!
Rampart Clarissa!

They embrace chastely

Clarissa Have you been busy at the House?

Rampart Frightfully! I saw Beaconsfield and discussed my proposed Bill for Total Temperance. It is my life's work, Clarissa, to see this bill through the House and become law.

Clarissa The bill has become a passion with you.

Rampart The consumption of alcohol by the lower classes is reaching alarming proportions, Clarissa. It must be stopped — for their own good! I have seen couples late at night walking home from public-houses — singing!

Clarissa Good heavens!

Rampart Thank goodness your eyes are saved from such scenes of degradation! I sometimes think that the British Empire is disintegrating!

Clarissa It makes me feel ill just to think about it. I never thought it possible!

Rampart Ah, but let us put such ugly thoughts from our minds for a moment! (*He takes Clarissa's hand*) Luncheon will be ready soon and as it is such a delightful day, I thought we could take a walk through St James's Park. The daffodils are in full bloom.

Clarissa In the midst of saving the country from itself you still find time to think up little pleasures for us to share! I am such a lucky woman!

Rampart 'Tis I who am the lucky one. For who else could I share my pleasures with?

Clarissa (*turning away*) But I must disappoint you, Archibald. I have received another message from my sister — my twin sister — to say that she is unwell again. She needs me by her side once more to nurse her back to full health.

Rampart I *am* sorry, Clarissa. Your sister's bouts of ill-health are becoming more frequent. It seems that every other month you spend with her. It seems strange that I have never met your twin sister. Are you very much alike?

Clarissa Mama could never tell us apart.

Rampart But she cannot be as lovely as you, my dear.

Clarissa But she is not as fortunate as I, Archibald. She is married to a poor tradesman in Bethnal Green and I fear it is the squalor in which they live that is ruining her health. Her husband—a brute of a man—frequents Music Halls and—how can I tell you —he drinks!

Rampart The poor woman! Then you must leave at once, hurry to her side before it is too late!

Clarissa You are such a treasure to allow me from your side.

Rampart I cannot bear to be parted from you for one second—but your sister needs you.

Clarissa It is the cross I have to bear, Archibald.

Rampart Of course, dearest, but do take care.

They embrace chastely once more

Clarissa I shall return as soon as I can, Archibald.

Clarissa exits

Rampart sits and studies a magazine

Branston enters and goes up to Rampart

Rampart straightens Branston, with suitable accompanying effects

Rampart What is it, Branston?

Branston Me Lord, there is a Lady without! (*He thumbs off* L)

Rampart (*raising his eyebrows*) Without what?

Branston There's a Lady in the 'all. And, me Lord, a curious thing. She is the spitting image of her Ladyship, why you could almost say she was her twin sister!

Rampart Twin sister? It cannot be!

Branston But for one difference, me Lord. Whilst her Ladyship is sweet, pure and chaste, this one is all—cor! (*He clenches his fists and shakes a leg*)

Rampart Branston! Behave yourself! Show the lady in, we must be prepared to help the less fortunate!

Branston staggers off

Rampart adjusts his necktie and collar

Branston enters and shakes a leg

Branston Mrs Cullet, me Lord! Cor!

Mrs Cullet enters L. *She wears a low-cut gown and is smoking through a long cigarette holder*

She drapes herself around the curtains, removes the holder, and speaks in a low, sultry voice

Mrs Cullet Why, hello there!

    Branston exits, muttering "Cor!"

Rampart (*gulping*) Hell—hello!
Mrs Cullet You must be my brother-in-law!
Rampart I am? I suppose I must be!

Mrs Cullet crosses to Rampart and runs her fingers up his necktie and tickles his chin

Mrs Cullet Not much of a welcome for such a close relative.
Rampart My wife has just left to visit you—we understood you were sick!
Mrs Cullet To the contrary! I am bursting with health! (*She thrusts closer to Rampart*)
Rampart (*eyeing her low-cut gown*) So I see!

Rampart makes an attempt to grab Mrs Cullet, but she twirls away leaving him grasping empty air

Mrs Cullet What do I call you, brother-in-law?
Rampart Call me? Oh, call me—Archie! What is your name?
Mrs Cullet Fiona. But you may call me whenever you wish! Shall we drink to our meeting?
Rampart Drink? You mean—(*he mimes raising a glass*)—but I never—
Mrs Cullet Just a small one. It will bring us closer together! (*She poses seductively*)

Rampart hesitates, then rings the bell

    Branston lurches on with a "Cor!"

Branston goes to Rampart and they walk down front

Rampart Branston, bring us—champagne!
Branston Champagne, me Lord? But you won't have strong drink in the 'ouse!
Rampart (*moving closer to Branston*) In the cellar! Behind the rocking horse!

Branston looks across at Mrs Cullet then at Rampart

Branston (*to the Audience*) Cor! (*He shakes a leg*)

Rampart nudges Branston on his way. Branston pauses when passing Mrs Cullet

Cor!

Branston exits

Rampart (*smiling*) Shall you be in town long?
Mrs Cullet (*meeting Rampart* C) It will depend.
Rampart On what?
Mrs Cullet On how well we get along together.
Rampart I'm sure we shall be great chums!

Mrs Cullet crosses to Rampart's right, holds him and lays him back. He supports himself with one hand

Mrs Cullet (*looking down at him*) Do you know, you are a very handsome man.

Rampart's and Mrs Cullet's heads are facing the entrance

Rampart (*out front*) Do you think so? (*He smiles*)
Mrs Cullet You send the blood coursing through my veins!
Rampart (*out front, smiling*) Do I really?
Mrs Cullet Kiss me, Archie!

They struggle to kiss, never quite making it

Branston enters with a tray and lurches towards them

Branston reacts to what he sees, whirling round a couple of times before finishing beside the couple, rattling the tray and glasses. Rampart and Mrs Cullet stand up and compose themselves, Mrs Cullet crossing L

Branston Good lord, me Lord!
Rampart Did you get it?
Branston (*behind his hand*) Did you?
Rampart Open it up, man!

Branston takes the bottle, placing the tray on the table. He struggles with the bottle. Rampart becomes impatient and grabs it from him

Rampart Give it here! (*He places the bottle between his legs, facing Branston, and struggles with the cork*

Branston (*to Mrs Cullet*) He can't get it out!

Mrs Cullet looks away amused. The cork comes out of the bottle and "shoots" Branston who falls over backwards and lays prostrate

Rampart (*filling glasses*) There we are! It sparkles just like your eyes, Fiona!

Mrs Cullet (*crossing to Rampart*) Will your wife be away for long, Archie?

Rampart (*handing her a glass*) Long enough, I hope!

Mrs Cullet Then let us drink — to us!

They link arms, holding glasses. Mrs Cullet pulls her arm close so that she drinks but Rampart cannot reach his glass. She drains her glass and allows Rampart to take a sip

   Mr Claude Cullet enters

Mr Cullet Aha!

Rampart sprays drink from his mouth

   Take your hands from that woman!

Mrs Cullet My husband!

Mr Cullet My Fiona!

Rampart My word!

Branston (*turning his head whilst still lying down*) My Lord!

Rampart Is this really your husband?

Mrs Cullet It is!

Rampart Then who are you?

Mrs Cullet I am his wife!

Rampart That means you are married! I should have known!

Mr Cullet Enough of this chitter-chatter! I've caught you red-handed! For years you have been slipping away under the pretence of nursing your sick sister! Now the game is up! You, sir, are nothing but a wife-stealer! My honour must be satisfied! Stand aside, Fiona!

Rampart (*studying his fingernails*) Throw the gentleman out, Branston!

Branston struggles to his feet and, staggering, goes through an exaggerated boxing routine before Mr Cullet. Mr Cullet snaps his fingers and Branston staggers backwards and collapses

Mr Cullet Now, sir! The question of my satisfaction! (*He pulls a pistol from his pocket*) I ask you to draw!

Rampart (*smiling weakly*) I do not possess a pistol!

Mrs Cullet crosses to the table and, lifting the magazine, takes up a pistol and hands it to Rampart

Mrs Cullet Try this one, Archie!

Rampart Very well! But I should warn you, sir, I have a very good eye!

Mr Cullet For the opposite sex it seems! I shall deal with you, sir, then it shall be your turn — *Mrs* Cullet!

Mrs Cullet Oh, save me, Archie! (*She clasps her head in her hands*)

Rampart Ready when you are, sir!

The two men stand back to back, then take three paces and turn and pull the triggers. Nothing happens. They pull and pull to no avail. Rampart adopts a fencing pose

On guard, sir!

Mr Cullet Your servant, sir!

They go through a fencing routine, thrusting and parrying until Rampart thrusts home with his pistol, a loud shot rings out and Cullet dies a glorious death

Mrs Cullet My poor husband! I must fetch help!

Mrs Cullet exits

Rampart blows into his pistol and puts it on the table, dusts himself down and rings the bell. Branston staggers to his feet

Rampart Branston, dispose of the body will you!

Branston Very good, me Lord!

Branston heaves Mr Cullet to his feet and drags him towards the exit, Cullet smiling broadly to the Audience

As they reach the exit Lady Clarissa enters and they collide

Branston and Mr Cullet stagger backwards and collapse side by side, centre stage. Clarissa crosses to Rampart

Clarissa Archibald! What is happening? I heard a gunshot! (*She gazes behind her, sees Cullet, and takes in the situation*) I see! My brother-in-law, Mr Claude Cullet, lies dead! A bottle of champagne—and two glasses! I know my twin sister has been here—you have had an adulterous affair with Fiona—her husband has caught you in the act—and you—you have killed him!

Rampart I'm sorry, Clarissa!

Clarissa That makes you an adulterous murderer, Archibald! And Branston was trying to conceal the body!

Rampart I'm afraid so, Clarissa!

Clarissa This will mean ruination for you, Archibald!

Rampart There is only one honourable way out, Clarissa!

Clarissa You don't mean—

Rampart Yes, it's the only way!

Clarissa If you must. (*She hands Rampart the pistol from the table*) It's such a waste!

Rampart I'm sorry, Clarissa!

Clarissa I forgive you, Archibald!

Rampart Goodbye, Clarissa!

Clarissa Goodbye, Archibald!

Rampart holds the pistol to his chest and pulls the trigger. The pistol fires and Rampart staggers around the stage in a spectacular death, finishing up lying by Cullet and Branston. Clarissa picks up the pistol between finger and thumb and places it under the magazines. She rings the bell and composes herself as Branston rises and staggers towards her

Branston You rang, your Ladyship?

Clarissa Yes, Branston. Will you dispose of the bodies?

Branston Very good, your Ladyship.

Clarissa reads a magazine whilst Branston heaves Cullet and Rampart to their feet and, arms over shoulder, walks them towards the exit. Both "bodies" smile broadly as they make their exits

   As they reach the exit a Police Constable enters, they collide

Branston, Cullet and Rampart stagger backwards and fall side by side, centre stage. The Constable walks over to them and nods his head at each body

Constable Hello! Hello! Hello! (*He turns to Clarissa*) May I ask what is agoin' on here, your Ladyship?

Clarissa Nothing, officer. We are just about to serve tea! One lump or two?

Constable I must warn you, your Ladyship, that I am here on hofficial business.

Clarissa Indeed? Is something amiss?

Constable I have come from the local nick—er—station, with a warrant for your Ladyship's arrest.

Clarissa Arrest? What nonsense!

Constable It says (*he reads from the warrant*) "That you did bigaman-noaniously marry Lord Rampart and Mr Claude Cullet, at the one and the same time, together." This is a serious offence, your Ladyship, and I must ask you to accompany me to the nick—er—station.

Clarissa But I am not guilty, officer. There lies the body of Lord Rampart. And there lies the body of Mr Claude Cullet, shot by Lord Rampart before he took his own life.

The Constable examines the bodies

Constable Oh, yes! They're dead all right!

Clarissa I can hardly be charged with bigamy when I am in fact, a widow—can I officer?

Constable It does alter the circumstances, your Ladyship! You are indeed a widow!

Clarissa (*sobbing*) And a lonely defenceless widow at that!

The Constable does a quick check on Clarissa and the dead bodies, and refers to his warrant

Constable Was this Lord Rampart, the art collector with a personal fortune of three million pounds?

Clarissa nods

And was Mr Claude Cullet the well-known door-knocker designer, also with a personal fortune of three million pounds?

Clarissa nods. The Constable does quick arithmetic on his fingers

That makes you a widow with a personal fortune of fi—six million pounds?

Clarissa It does. And being a rich defenceless widow, I am in need of comfort and protection. (*She smiles at the Constable*)

Constable (*tearing the warrant into shreds*) Who says a policeman's lot is not a happy one! (*He lifts Clarissa up in his arms and walks towards the exit*) Evening all!

The Constable and Clarissa exit

CURTAIN

FURNITURE AND PROPERTY LIST

Only essential furniture is listed. Other items may be added as required

On stage: Small table. *On it:* hand bell, cigarettes, matches, magazines,
concealed pistol
Sofa
Curtains at window

Off stage: Tray. *On it:* two glasses, bottle of champagne

Personal: **Rampart:** gold hunter watch
Mrs Cullet: cigarette holder
Mr Cullet: pistol
Police Constable: warrant

LIGHTING PLOT

Interior setting

No cues

EFFECTS PLOT

No cues

MARIA MARTEN
or
MURDER IN THE RED BARN

A Victorian Melodrama

CHARACTERS:
Maria Marten, a simple country maid
William Corder, a villainous Squire
Sailor Jack, of the Royal Navy
Constable, long arm of the law

SCENE 1   The cross roads
SCENE 2   The Red Barn

Time: Victorian

Running time approximately 13 minutes

MARIA MARTEN

Scene 1

The cross roads

Maria enters, weeping. She wears a black dress with a white apron and mop-cap. A shawl covers her shoulders and a nicely-rounded tummy explains the reason for her tears

Maria Alas! What shall I do? I, poor Maria Marten, a simple country maid, have been wronged by the Squire, William Corder. And will not the chee-ild that I bear be the result of our clandestine union? But he shall marry me yet! He has made a promise to me and I shall see that he keeps his word (*with her hands on her tummy*) — why — he's just *got* to. Until I walked out with William I was an innocent young maid — and now —? But what of my sweetheart, Sailor Jack? If only he were here, this would never have happened. But he has been gone these two years and I fear he will never return! (*She weeps*) Ah! I hear footprints! Someone comes! (*She looks off* L)

Corder enters R

Corder Ah — ha!

Maria jumps. Corder returns hisses and catcalls from the Audience

My dearest Maria!

He takes Maria's hand and kisses it. His kisses run up her arm until Maria pulls away

Maria Oh, William! How you excite me!

Corder But Maria, 'tis you who excite me. I am drawn again and again to your side.

Maria But you are a sophisticated man, used to city life — what can you see in me, a simple country girl?

Corder 'Tis your unspoilt country charm that attracts me, Maria.

He makes to embrace her but she pulls away

Maria Have a care, William. My mother or father might see us!

Corder (*aside*) Meddling old fools! You have told nobody of our affair?

Maria shakes her head

  Our little secret?

Maria Why, of course not, William. You told me to keep me trap shut—and I have!

Corder Good girl! Good girl! (*He pats her arm. Out front*) Thank goodness for that!

Maria (*coyly*) Willi—um!

Corder (*sharply*) What is it, you stup—(*softly*) yes, Maria, what is it?

Maria examines the third finger of her left hand

Maria William, when are you going to keep your promise to me?

Corder Promise? Promise? Now, what did I promise my little Maria? Hm?

Maria Why, William! You promised to marry me and make an honest woman of me—as soon as you knew about—(*she pats her tummy*)

Corder Shush, girl! (*He looks about. Out front*) Stupid creature will blow the gaff to the whole wide world! (*To Maria, with charm*) Maria, did I not tell you that any news of our—er—affair would jeopardize several lucrative ventures that I am engaged upon? Now, you would not stand in the way of my business career, would you, Maria? Hm?

Maria Of course not, William. But I feel that the time is fast approaching when the whole world will know about you and me. (*Tapping her tummy*) If you see what I mean!

Corder (*out front*) Curses! Why did I become entangled with such a stupid creature? (*He walks* R) I must think! I must have time to think!

Maria That's just it, William. We ain't got time—(*she counts on her fingers*)—not a lot, anyway! It's make-your-mind-up time!

Corder (*reaching a decision*) We shall do it tonight! Maria, pack a valise! We shall leave on the night coach for London!

Maria London! Oh, William!

Corder Yes. And we shall be married tomorrow!

Maria claps her hands with joy

Maria I must run and tell my mother and father — and my sister Nellie!

She tries to break L but Corder grasps her wrist and pulls her back

Corder Stay! Stay, Maria! (*Out front*) Will she never learn? (*Calmly*) For the time being, our marriage must remain a secret —

Maria But I want to tell everyone, William! A simple country girl like me — marrying the rich, handsome Squire —

Corder We shall tell them, Maria, but later. This news would —

Maria (*reciting in flat monotone*) — jeopardize several lucrative ventures that you are engaged upon.

Corder Exactly! Now, you wouldn't want to marry a broken, penniless man, would you?

Maria (*indifferently*) Wouldn't bother me, William. I been broke and penniless all me life!

Corder So, pack your belongings and meet me tonight — at the Red Barn!

Maria Ooh! I ain't going there again!

Corder Why not?

Maria Huh! I remember what happened the last time!

Corder But this will be for the last time, there will be no coming back! Ha! Ha! Ha!

Maria I don't want to come back here, William.

Corder (*out front*) She won't. After tonight, I shall be free! (*To Maria*) Remember. Tonight at the Red Barn!

Maria puckers up her lips, closes her eyes and reaches forward

> *Corder swirls his cape, twirls his moustache and sweeps off L, ignoring her*

Maria I don't know if I can really trust my lover! If only I had someone to confide in! If only Sailor Jack were here! (*She sobs*)

> *To the first eight bars of "A Life on the Ocean Wave" on comes Sailor Jack from R. He wears a sailor's uniform and sports a fine bushy beard held on by elastic. He carries a kit-bag and a bird cage. He stands to attention and salutes as the music finishes*

Jack   I'm Sailor Jack!
              And I've just come back
              From sailing o'er the foam!

Never more, to leave the shore,
It's good to be back home! (Boom! Boom!)

He does a little skip and stamps his feet, saluting, to the "Boom, Boom" which should be played by drums or piano

(*Moving to Maria*) Hello, Maria! Come on, give us a kiss!

Jack takes Maria's arm but she pulls away

Maria 'Ere, you let go! You saucy seaman! Have you know I don't go round kissing strange sailors!

Jack But I'm not a strange sailor!

Maria You're the strangest sailor I've ever seen!

Jack But, Maria. 'Tis me! Your own Sailor Jack! Home from sea — home for good!

Maria (*turning away*) Garn off with you! You ain't *my* Sailor Jack! *My* Jack never had a beard!

Jack I made a promise never to shave until I saw you again. That was two long years ago. Beneath these whiskers I am the same Sailor Jack! 'Ere! Remember behind the haystack, Maria?

He nudges Maria, who peers at him

Maria (*out front*) It can't be! But is it? (*She pulls his beard down revealing his face*) It is! It's my own Sailor Jack!

Maria releases the beard which flies back, but stays under Jack's chin. He has difficulty refitting the beard in place. They embrace warmly, Jack pulling the beard down to kiss Maria

Jack I have sailed the seven seas and seen the wonders of the world, but now — I have come home to marry you, Maria! (*He beams*)

Maria (*moving down front*) Oh! What shall I tell my Sailor Jack? (*She looks across to Jack*) I can't marry you right away, Jack. You'll have to wait a little while.

Jack Why?

Maria Er — (*an idea!*) 'Cos it's Lent!

Jack Well, when will you get it back?

Maria Oh, Jack! The truth is I have been walking out with the Squire, William Corder.

Jack (*leaping back with alarm*) Not Cocksure Corder? He's a proper Don Juan, he is! Why, a simple country girl like you would be helpless in his grasp!

Maria I soon found that out, didn't I?

Jack looks aghast at Maria's figure

He brought me a bunch of daffodils and asked me to meet him in the Red Barn!

Jack The Red Barn?

Maria nods

The next six lines are said very quickly

You didn't?
Maria I did!
Jack He didn't?
Maria He did!
Jack You're not?
Maria I am!

They turn back to back, Maria sobs, Jack strokes his beard

Jack What a welcome home!

They turn to the front

Maria What am I to do, Jack? He told me to meet him in the Red Barn tonight, and we go to London to be married tomorrow!

Jack You know what will happen if you meet him in the Red Barn tonight, don't you?

Maria (*eagerly*) Will I be helpless in his grasp again?

Jack Worse than that, Maria! It could be—(*he mimes strangulation*)

Maria Oh, Jack! What am I to do?

Jack (*taking charge*) Nothing, Maria! You meet him in the Red Barn as arranged. But *I* shall be there, to protect you—and to settle my score with Squire Corder!

Jack turns back his cuffs and adopts a boxer's stance, fists clenched. Maria looks adoringly on as

the CURTAIN *falls*

Scene 2

The Red Barn

The interior of the Barn is gloomy. A pile of hay is in the centre of the stage

Maria enters from L, *clutching a small bag, her shawl wrapped tightly round her shoulders*

Maria But it's dark and creepy! But I have nothing to fear, my Sailor Jack is a'coming to protect me. Hark! I hear his footprints now! (*She puts her hand to her left ear*)

Corder enters R

Corder Ah, ha!

Maria William! (*She holds her bosom*) Why, you made my heart miss a beat!

Corder (*out front*) Her heart will miss many a beat before this night is through! (*To Maria*) Maria! How ravishing you look! (*Privately*) Yuck!

Maria See! I have my valise packed for the journey!

Corder (*looking both ways*) Did anyone see you come down the lane?

Maria Not a soul.

Corder That is good, Maria.

Maria But why so secretive, William? If we are to be married tomorrow —

Corder There will be no marriage!

Maria But the journey to London?

Corder The only journey you will take will be to — oblivion! Ha! Ha! Ha! Ha!

Maria But why, William? I don't quite understand.

Corder Because you are a millstone round my neck! Dragging me down! Holding me back! I am an ambitious man, Maria, you have no place in my future plans, so — tonight, you die! (*He advances upon Maria, his hands reaching for her throat*)

Maria (*recoiling*) No! No!

Corder Yes! Yes!

Maria Spare me! Spare my chee-ild!

Corder Never! You die!

He grasps her by the throat and slowly they make their way behind the pile of hay. Corder forces Maria down and, as she disappears behind the hay, Corder releases his hold and begins to rise. Maria's hand rises from behind the hay and beckons him down, he stoops and throttles her again. He rises and Maria's hand again beckons him for more. As he rises this time her hand appears but flutters and falls with a loud thud. Corder dusts his coat and walks to the front

Corder 'Tis done! The deed is done! I have thrust off my shackles and I am free! (*He looks back at the pile of hay*) God rest her soul, but there was no other way. I have shrugged off that stupid wench at last! Now I can pursue my wicked ways without further distraction! But first — to bury the body! (*He goes over to the pile of hay*)

The first eight bars of "A Life on the Ocean Wave" are heard as Jack enters and stands to attention

Jack   Not so fast, shipmate!
Corder   Curses! Who are you?
Jack   I'm Sailor Jack!
(*out front*)   And I've just come back
                From sailing o'er the foam!
                Never more to leave the shore
                It's good to be back home! (Boom! Boom!)

He skips, stamps his feet and salutes as before

Corder   Maria's sweetheart? It can't be! Sailor Jack had no beard!
Jack   Beneath these whiskers I am the same Sailor Jack!
Corder   It can't be! But is it?

Corder pulls the beard down revealing Jack's face

   It is!

Corder releases the beard which flies up and returns over Jack's face. Temporarily blinded, Jack wanders around the stage. The Chairman could face Jack in the right direction. Jack refits his beard, but is disturbed by this unexpected turn of events and "fluffs" his next line

Jack   I have a squaw to settle with you, Squire — a Squire to settle with you, squaw — a *score* to settle with you, Squire!
Corder   Indeed? I have not time for sea-faring fools! (*He turns away*)

Jack I know about your affair with Maria. And the result!

Corder (*out front*) Curse the wench! She blabbed! He is but a simple seaman, I shall talk him round!

Jack rolls up his right sleeve, clenches his fist and shows it to the Audience

Jack (*out front*) This'll be the one that'll do it!

Jack poses to throw an almighty punch at Corder as the Squire meets him C but, putting an arm around Jack's shoulder, Corder walks him across R

Corder As Squire of this village, it is my duty to be of help to girls as unfortunate as Maria. Yes! That's it! I was helping her! (*He smiles at Jack*)

Jack Oh, yes? From what I hear, you've been helping *yourself*! (*He adopts a boxing stance*) Come on, you wicked devil—put 'em up!

Corder (*stepping back*) You meddling matelot! I'll soon deal with you! For you shall join Maria—in her grave!

Jack Not I! 'Tis you for Davey Jones's locker!

They both spar, then step forward and come chest to chest and throw punches across each other's shoulders, accompanied by grunts and shouts

   A Constable enters R

Constable Hello! Hello! Hello! What's a'goin' on here?

Corder Seize this rascal, Constable! He attacks me for my money! (*He holds Jack's shoulder by finger and thumb, almost lifting Jack off his feet*)

Jack Not I! This devil has admitted murdering my sweetheart, Maria Marten, here in the Red Barn!

Constable Oh, yes? And who might you be?

Corder releases Jack

Jack   I'm Sailor Jack!
               And I've just come back
               From sailing o'er the foam!
               Never more, to leave the shore
               It's good to be back home! (Boom! Boom!)

On the "Boom! Boom!" this time all three actors skip and stamp feet. Jack salutes

The Constable peers closely at Jack

Constable You're not the Sailor Jack I used to know — Jack never had whiskers!

Jack (*wearily*) Beneath these whiskers, I am the same Sailor Jack!

The Constable peers again

Constable (*out front*) Can it be? Is it? (*He pulls down Jack's beard*) It is!

The Constable releases the beard (which flies up covering Jack's face) and shakes Jack's hand at the same time. In the confusion Corder begins to creep off L

Corder Now's me chance to escape!

Constable Not so fast, Squire! (*He crosses to Corder and takes his arm*) Where is Maria?

Corder shrugs

Take a look around, Jack!

Jack goes the long way round before reaching the pile of hay and walking behind it. He trips over Maria's body and takes several steps before doing a double-take and returning to the hay. He stoops, then rises, holding Maria's hand. He lets her hand go and as it falls it hits the ground with a loud thud. Jack puts an arm across his face with grief

Jack There she lies! My little Maria! Gone for ever!

Corder Another minute and I could have buried the body!

Constable A confession, eh? You come along a'me! Your philandering days are over, *Mister* Corder! (*As he turns to take Corder off he smiles at Jack*) It's good to have you back again, Jack! Good luck, old son!

The Constable marches Corder off

Jack comes down front as they leave

Jack Good luck, he says! And my dear Maria, gone for ever!

Jack cries. As he wipes away the tears with his beard a baby's cries are heard, becoming louder. Jack stops crying and wanders round the stage before reaching the hay. He leans over to where Maria lies, then stands upright holding a small bundle in his arms. He comforts the child

Cootchie cootchie coo!
Cootchie cootchie coo!

The baby stops crying

That's better! (*He tickles the baby's chest, holding his beard at the same time. He tries to pull his head back but the baby seems to be holding his beard and will not let go*) Let go! Leggo! You little monster! (*He snatches his head back, displacing the beard once more*)

Maria's face appears from behind the hay. She rises unsteadily to her feet

Maria   Jack! Oh, my Sailor Jack!

Jack meets her and walks her down front

Jack   Why, Maria! Look what I got here! 'Tis a little baby!
Maria   Is it a boy or girl?

Jack holds the baby to his ear and shakes it

Jack (*smiling*) It's a boy!

Maria takes the baby and they link arms

Maria   My Sailor Jack, has just come back
                  My life is filled with laughter!
                  Him and me, and baby's three
                  We'll be happy ever after! (Boom! Boom!)

They skip and stamp on the "Boom! Boom!"

CURTAIN

Curtain call tableau: Jack with beard over his face; Constable holding the baby; Squire and Maria in very passionate embrace

FURNITURE AND PROPERTY LIST

SCENE 1

No scenery required

Personal: **Jack:** kitbag, bird cage, beard on elastic

SCENE 2

Set: Pile of hay

Personal: **Maria:** bag

LIGHTING PLOT

Scene 1

To open: outdoor lighting
No cues

SCENE 2

To open: gloomy interior
No cues

EFFECTS PLOT

Cue 1   As Jack cries   (Page 55)
           Baby cries. Stop when ready

MADE AND PRINTED IN GREAT BRITAIN BY
LATIMER TREND & COMPANY LTD PLYMOUTH
MADE IN ENGLAND